I0829614

Healthy Relationships

Compromise Leads To Failure

Destiny S. Harris

...

. . .

Copyright

. . .

. . .

A Gift For You

Thank you for taking the time to read this book. As a token of my appreciation, here is a gift to you.

I give away free books daily. Here's how to get your free books today:

Step 1: Visit amazon.com/author/destinyharris

Step 2: Filter books by "Price: Low to High"

Step 3: Download available free eBooks

. . .

...

Table of Contents

...

. . .

Quick Bit

Thank you for taking the time to read this book.

My hope is that you leave at least 1% better than before you read this book and walk away with at least one takeaway.

I'd like to graciously ask that you help me by leaving a <u>review</u> of this book; your feedback helps me write better books and helps others get a glimpse of the book.

With Kindness,
Destiny

...

. . .

Chapter 1

Keep The End In Mind

Who is the person I'm dating today, and is the person someone I could date long-term if they never change or evolve?

Far too many enter relationships with people in hopes they will change this or that.

If you can't fully accept a person for who they are today, **and be happy and at peace with them,** walk away. The sooner you can walk away, the better. Because the longer you stay and engage, the more likely your emotions will pile up, making it more difficult to walk away.

People committed to personal growth naturally evolve. But many people aren't committed to personal growth or even open to it. Things don't usually get better in a relationship unless you have two people committed to improving things. Most relationships gradually decay over time. People naturally decay over time.

So, if you can't accept the person for who they are today 10 or 20 years from now, what makes you think you'll be able to accept it down the road when there will likely be even more stuff you don't like?

Pay attention to how you feel around a person. Do you feel more peace or stress? Do you feel you must push them to improve themselves, or are they proactive? Does the person make you smile and add happiness to your life, or do they make you uncomfortable and uneasy? Do you feel you're compromising your values and standards with this person, or are you aligned?

. . .

...

Chapter 2

Adaptable or Rigid

You can have two rigid people come together, and it works because they're rigid in all the right ways, and it harmonizes.

One rigid person can come together with an adaptable person, which works because the adaptable person is easygoing and doesn't get flustered with a rigid person.

But when you have two rigid people who are unwilling to harmonize, it spells disaster.

Always pay attention to how flexible and adaptable a person is, not only with you, but with life and other people. Are they tolerant of inconvenience? Do they get upset when plans change? Is their personality easy going? Are they easy to be around when they're stressed? Are they open-minded? Do they make you feel like your wants and desires are important? Do they care about your needs and prioritize them?

Adaptable people are much easier to be with in the long run.

. . .

...

Chapter 3

You or Your Body

If you're looking for casual sex, you'll find it. If you're looking for something serious, you'll also find it.

Sex doesn't inhibit healthy relationships, but delaying sex can potentially increase the quality of a relationship.

Sex is something that should always be seen as an enhancement to a relationship. If you aren't happy being with or around the person unless you're being physical, you're setting yourself up for failure.

When two people are dedicated to getting to know each other and not each other's bodies, they can make a sounder decision as to whether or not the relationship makes logical sense. Knowing someone's body should always be a last priority.

What are the person's goals, dreams, ambitions, quirks, and successes. How does the person live? Who are they? Who are they evolving into / where are they headed?

The person you enter a relationship with should be similarly minded. Integrating sex into a situation doesn't destroy the opportunity to know a person, but it can delay or negatively affect the process.

Establishing a sound foundation of friendship can create a healthier outcome.

Most rush into the physical aspect of a relationship, which mitigates the quality of it.

. . .

. . .

Chapter 4

Similar Values

Having similar hobbies can help you and your partner thrive, but two people can find and build new hobbies together.

Values is what matters most. For example, I place a high value on holistic health (i.e., emotional, mental, physical, spiritual, and financial, professional) and a commitment to personal development.

If a person doesn't share these values, it's difficult for me to connect with them, which means the relationship or dating situation has an automatic end date.

Values Trump Hobbies
Values > Hobbies

I know it's great when you're dating a person and you like all the same things, but if they don't share the same values as you, you will struggle in the short or long-term with the relationship.

Values is what truly connects two people together when you want a quality outcome.

Are you both on a similar life track? Do you both want kids? Do you both value family? Do you both stay active? Do you both value traveling and new experiences? Are you both spiritual or religious? Do you both enjoy saving or spending money? Do you both align financially and how you manage money? How do you both view sex? What does a relationship mean to each of you? When things are going good or bad, are you both open to counseling to ensure it stays in a healthy place?

Focus on values, not hobbies.

. . .

. . .

Chapter 5

Financial Alignment

A lot of people wait to ask questions concerning money, but it's a conversation that should be held early on.

If you're a spender and the other person is a saver, what does that look like?

How much debt is shared between the two of you? What are their intentions to pay off their debt?

Are they investing for their future or living in the moment?

Do they make abrupt and illogical purchases?

Do they live below or above their means?

What are their financial goals? How much do they earn? Do their earnings align with your earnings? Do they live a life that correlates with the vision you have for your life?

These might seem like hard questions to dive into, but they're some of the most important questions you'll ask that can help you make more logical decisions.

When you enter a relationship, you're marrying the financial habits of the person. If you're uncomfortable "marrying" the finances of the other person, think twice before proceeding.

...

. . .

Chapter 6

Compromise

Certain people will come into your life that help you see how much value you place on your values.

I'm an active person. There have been amazing people that have come into my life that aren't active, and I tried to learn if it made sense, but in the end, I could never fully harmonize with them because they didn't maintain an active lifestyle.

Now I know, health is a value I cannot compromise on. This is how I see it: If a person isn't taking care of themselves well enough, how can they ever take care of me? At some point, I'll likely have to care for them.

People who live inactive lifestyles and don't consume an overall healthy diet frequently deal with preventable health issues and low energy. But moreover, a person who doesn't value their health doesn't fully value themselves; they also demonstrate a lack of discipline, which carries over into every area of their lives.

Health is one of the most critical keys to success. A person naturally prioritizes it or doesn't.

So back to my original statement:

Certain people will come into your life that help you see how much value you place on your values.

If you value financial discipline, people will come into your life that lack financial discipline to test your values. Do you value financial discipline and success as much as you think or are you willing to compromise?

Once you're unwilling to settle on your values, the universe brings people in your life that meet or exceed your standards because it respects the fact that you know what you want without hesitation.

. . .

...

Chapter 7

Effort

The small, medium, and big stuff count.

Does a person pay attention to the things you say, like, and do? Does a person put in effort to cater to your likes, wants, and needs? Does a person consistently put their best foot forward? Does a person want to make you happy? Does a person make you feel valued, loved, cherished, and like the only person in the world? Does a person make you feel safe? Does a person make you feel like every moment spent with them is worth it?

Effort counts.

People who invest effort and energy easily distinguish themselves from those who don't.

You can't teach a person effort and you shouldn't make it your job to.

A person will either find you valuable enough to invest effort or won't. And don't take it personal when people don't invest time, effort, and energy into you.

The right people will always be sure to invest the right effort into you. Effort also will help you weed out the people who don't belong in a long-term situation with you.

Consistent effort is the loudest communicator.

Can a person consistently invest effort over the long-haul? Not just the beginning.

. . .

. . .

Chapter 8

Date Multiple People

Popular advice is to date multiple people at once, which is true, and here's why:

1. When you're dating, avoid getting caught up on one person too early in a situation.

2. In the early stages, it's important to assess how a person makes you feel.

You might think you're happy or on cloud 9 until you meet someone that takes you to cloud 15.

You can't comprehend what cloud 15 is unless you date multiple people.

Dating multiple people is doing your due diligence to ensure you're learning your wants, needs, and preferences for a partner. It can be difficult or slow to learn these things when you jump from one relationship to the next or only date one person at a time.

Get out there and notice how each person makes you feel.

Notice how you act and engage with different people. You'll be surprised at what you learn about yourself when you really put yourself out there and go on several dates.

Yes, it's not always easy to do this, and there might be some fear and anxiety related, but dating or spending time with different people (without sex), can help you learn what you value and want in a relationship.

. . .

...

Chapter 9

Communication and Reliability

Is it easy to be yourself and communicate to the other person?

Do you **enjoy** consistently communicating with the person, or do you feel apprehensive about communicating freely and enjoyably with the person?

Does the person make you feel safe when you communicate with them?

Does the person initiate quality conversation and ask questions that help you both learn more about each other?

Is the communication dual-sided or one-sided?

Communication is critical for two parties to effectively have a successful relationship.

If both parties can't communicate, failure is inevitable.

On top of this, is there trust?

Do you both lie about small, medium, or big things with each other?

Do you both bring integrity to the situation?

Integrous communication creates a solid foundation for a healthy relationship.

. . .

. . .

Chapter 10

It's Right When It's Right

It seems like it takes people forever (or extended time) to determine if the wrong person is right for them.

But many know relatively quickly when a person is right for them, and I'm not talking about hormones and emotions telling us a person is right; I'm talking about logic.

You'll know a person is right for you when you don't have to compromise your values, they add value to your life, you experience peace, and time has been invested in the relationship without the physical aspect introduced to make you feel confident that it is the right move.

When a person is right for you, you experience little doubt, and the relationship is relatively smooth sailing.

Relationships aren't actually supposed to be hard; they're not always easy, but it should make sense.

When you're intentionally dating, keep the end in mind, consistently reflect your experiences with the other person, and stay in tune with your emotions, mind, and body.

When we pay attention to how we respond to people, we can learn a lot.

Your romantic partner is the most important relationship you'll ever have because of how close and intertwined the relationship is.

A person either helps you progress or recede in life.

Be sure you date people that lift you up, but also be sure you're in a place to do the same.

Everything you're hoping to receive and experience from someone should also be something you can offer them.

...

...

Thank You For Reading

Thank you for reading this book.

Stay loved, blessed, lucky, favored, aware, joyous, enlightened, and committed to bettering yourself.

. . .

. . .

The End.

. . .

...

About Destiny S. Harris

Destiny S. Harris' goal is to positively inspire, cultivate, elevate, and educate the minds of individuals across the globe through her writing.

Creating (whether books, courses, articles, poetry, or music) has always been Destiny's thing, not to mention health & fitness and all things entrepreneurial.

Destiny published her first book, "Beauty Secrets for Girls," at age 11 and her second book, "Don't Wait Until It's Too Late," at age 12.

Destiny obtained three degrees in Psychology, Political Science, & Women's Studies. She also started her own music teaching business at the age of 14, which she led for over ten years. In addition, she has been teaching academic, career, and personal development topics to thousands of students and readers since 2004.

Outside of writing, Destiny loves and enjoys many activities: reading, weightlifting, walking, biking, traveling, football (and sports in general), dogs, animals, food, classic movies, quality and new experiences, mountain, and ocean views, sleeping, plants, and nature.

Check out her work, leave a review, share your thoughts with your friends and family, and participate in a movement: **Serving others through self-education (books).**

Complete the Steps To Get Free eBooks:

Step 1: Go to

amazon.com/author/destinyharris

Step 2: Filter books by "Price: Low to High"

Step 3: Download available free books

...

...

Connect W/ Destiny S. Harris

Please reach out and stay in touch. Start a conversation today @ destinyh.com

. . .

...

Free Gifts!

Access courses & free eBooks at the link below:

destinyh.com

...

Please Leave A Review

If this book impacts you in some way, please let me know by dropping a review on it.

I write better books with **your** input.

. . .

Tell Me What You Want

I've written many books, but if you don't see what you're looking for or need, get in touch with me via my website, articles, comments, or reviews, and let me know what you're looking for so I can create it for you. I'm here to serve.

Destiny

. . .

. . .